FREEDOM'S TRAIL

SPRINGBORO AND THE UNDERGROUND RAILROAD

HELEN SPROAT

White Dog Books

ISBN# 978-0-9842351-4-8

First Edition: May 2010

Cover art by Karen Ware

Cover design by Ron D'Allessandris

Printed on Acid free paper.

FOREWORD

In the years that I have been leading Springboro's Underground Railroad tours, I have found myself more and more involved in these wonderful stories. I am not a native of this historic town, but I have spent 40 years of my life here and take as much pride in the local heritage as I would if these brave people were my forefathers. To me, these are stories of such determination and courage that I am proud to pass them on and to live in the town where these events took place.

Don Ross, then president of the Springboro Area Historical Society first enlisted me to help with the tour program he had established. Don is one of those quiet leaders who make people eager to join in their projects. He gave me a folder of pages written in his bold calligraphy, and I read the results of the research he had been doing since he retired from being the most popular teacher at Springboro High School. The information I relate to you now is based almost entirely on Don's research. I have "read up on" related topics, but I am only passing on Don's work.

When Don left Springboro, Carol Stone took over the tour responsibility. Carol, aka Grace Prudhoe, the escaped slave, had developed a wonderful first-person presentation, which was so believable that people felt a compulsion to go up to her and hug her after the program. As I worked with her, I found myself presenting the history of slavery and having Carol walk in quietly, in costume, and give her talk as Grace, herself. It was very moving and not soon to be forgotten.

Then Carol also had to move away, which left me in charge. Having learned from these two inspired people, how could I not love telling these stories? This is not just history; this is the history of this special town, and we walk down the street and stand in front of buildings which were once Underground Railroad depots. The stories I tell are very important to us today. They tell of slaves, fleeing desperately from their bondage, and with no reason to trust any white man. In Springboro they meet the Quakers, dedicated to the equality of all men and willing to risk breaking the law to help these fugitives to safety. The slaves were welcomed quietly to the Quaker homes, fed and perhaps given warm clothing and then hidden away for a day. Occasionally people came searching for the slaves, a danger for both the fugitives and their guardians. The slaves would have to be hidden in some tiny hiding place, -crowded, perhaps damp and dark, - and often locked in. Their freedom depended upon their ability to trust and wait, while the Quakers also had to trust that the slaves would lie very silently so as not to give themselves away to the bounty hunters. If they were found out, the slaves would be sent back to their masters and the Quakers would be arrested for aiding a criminal.

This year the Springboro Area Historical Society Trustees decided that it was time to have a folder put together by each officer or Committee Chair, telling his or her duties, with all contacts and schedules. This will make future transitions smoother and easier. I decided to go a little further with the tour information and put the notes into narrative form. This will also serve as an educational pamphlet or even a souvenir of a visit to Springboro. I hope you enjoy your tour.

A BRIEF HISTORY OF SLAVERY IN AMERICA

Slavery has been with us since the dawn of civilization. As soon as man began living in communities, quarrels arose with other towns or states over water, game, whatever. Battles followed, small-scale wars, and captives were taken. These were the first slaves, to be used for barter or to work for their captors. The glory days of Egypt, Athens and Rome saw their magnificent pyramids and buildings built and served by slaves. Passages in The Bible tell how one was expected to treat his slaves. With the development of shipping and world trade in Europe, the slave trade became well established north of the Mediterranean as well.

When the first settlers came to America, they brought slaves to help clear the land and build the houses. The poor and highly religious Pilgrims did not own slaves, but the well-to-do men who founded the early Virginia settlements of Jamestown and Williamsburg surely did. The early settlers also tried to enslave the Native Americans, but this proved to be a frustrating practice. The local Indians knew the land so much better than the white man and were far too resourceful to be kept as slave laborers. When the opportunity arose, most simply slipped away into the forest.

The colonists also had indentured servants to help them. Most of these were young men and women from England or Ireland. They longed for the opportunity of life in this new land but could not afford to pay for passage on a ship to America. Ship Captains would offer them passage in return for the right to sell their "indentures". Upon their arrival in Boston or Philadelphia, someone who needed a carpenter's assistant or housemaid would pay the Captain for that passage and the young worker would become a sort of temporary slave until he or she had worked long enough to pay off that debt. It usually took 3 to 5 years, but there were definite rules involved and papers signed. At the end of his indenture, the worker received a small sum of money and two suits of clothes to start him out. Part of the arrangement was that he would be taught a trade during his indenture, so that he was ready to join the workforce. This might be only "farming" for a man or "housewifery" for a woman, but when their indentures were over, most of these determined young people did very well on their own. The courts often placed young orphans as indentured servants, sometimes in the home of a relative, where they were fed, educated and worked until they came of age.

Some slaves lived fairly comfortable lives. Often a family would own two slaves, a husband and wife. They would live in the house with their owners and share in their day to day lives. The man would help his master in his work and be a "handyman" around the house, while his wife would help clean house, cook or care for the children. They were generally well treated and comfortable. The children called them "Aunt" or "Uncle" and considered them part of the family. They were appreciated and often loved. ("Aunt Jemima" and "Uncle Ben" were obviously fine cooks and "Uncle Remus" entertained the children with his wonderful stories.)

The slave structure which developed in the early American south was very different. The southern planters had bought huge tracts of land, which was inexpensive and was originally considered poor farm land. Most was in woodland, - huge pine forests, - and the men who first bought it didn't look beyond harvesting the timber. They knew that they could not grow the corn or wheat that were the staples of northern agriculture, as the climate was too warm and dry. However, once they had cleared some of the forested fields, they found that this southern soil grew different crops, which could not grow in the north, and so would sell for a good price. Flax did well, as did indigo, for dye, and even the boggy lowlands grew rice. But the best crop of all was cotton. The northern mills had plenty of wool for warm winter clothes, but the cotton for summer clothing had to be imported from Mexico or the Caribbean Islands. There was a ready market in the north or in Europe for all the cotton the southern plantations could produce.

The problem with cotton was that it was very labor intensive. In those days, before mechanization, everything in the cultivation of cotton had to be done by hand. The fields had to be cleared and plowed, the cotton planted and weeded and harvested, and then the crop had to be cleaned and baled and taken to market. Even after 1793, when Eli Whitney's invention of the cotton gin did ease the job of cleaning the raw cotton, most of the work was hand labor and the plantation owners could not hire enough workers to tend all those huge fields. Slavery was, to them, the logical answer. By the mid

1700s, there were slaves in South and Central America, Mexico and all the Caribbean Islands. Brazil alone had more slaves than the United States ever had! The slave trade, already strong between Africa and Europe, turned to the west and brought thousands of African slaves to the southern states.

To the planters, their slaves were a necessary expenditure. Their manual labor was what made the plantation successful, and slaves were treated about as well as a good draft horse. They had shelter and food and medical attention, but only as much as was necessary to keep them healthy and able to work hard. They were bought and sold as needed and, naturally, were more valuable, and productive, if healthy. The slave's wishes or feelings were almost never considered. Slaves were paired up by the master, not by who loved whom, but by who would produce strong, healthy children together. Families were then broken down ruthlessly with the sale of husband, wife or children. It was all part of the business of the plantation.

THE LIFE OF A SLAVE

Consider how the African went from free man to slave. Generally his life in Africa was in a tribal village or rural area. Most were farmers; they understood planting and harvesting or hunting for their own families or tribal groups. Most were captured by other tribes, who would then sell them to the slavers. They were taken with their entire tribe, men, women and children, even the tribal chiefs, and marched off to the sea, where they were imprisoned in stockades until the ship arrived. The slave ships had many decks, so close together that a man couldn't sit up, and the captives were packed in like sardines. They lay side by side, head to toe and chained in place. The trip to America took about a month. The slavers knew that if the slaves were released briefly each day for a little fresh air and exercise, they would be healthier and bring a better price, but even on these more humane ships, disease spread like wildfire on those crowded decks. It was not unusual to lose from 30 to 50% of the slaves on the voyage.

Upon arrival in America, the slave would be sold at auction and taken away, with a chain around his neck, to a plantation which he would probably never leave. His family members who had survived the journey would be sold to other owners. He would probably never see them again. He could not speak or understand English; quite often there was no one on the plantation who could understand him, as tribal languages differ. He learned English by trying to do as the other slaves did, because an overseer would whip him if he didn't obey an order. The work was exhausting and again he learned by trying to keep up with the others. A slave family had probably been told to take him to live with them, so he would have a roof over his head, but there was never enough food. He would be given two shirts (made of spoiled or unsalable cloth) and two pairs of cheap, scratchy "linsey-woolsey" pants; he had to make them last a year.

Most slaves, men and women, worked as "field hands". They were taken to work in the fields for long days, sun-up to sun-down. In winter or early spring they dug out tree stumps from the cleared fields and then plowed and smoothed the soil, using teams of horses or oxen. Planting the cotton seeds was easy; that was women's work. Two women would plant a field of cotton. One carried a pointed stick and the other had the bag of cotton seeds. They walked single file the length of the field and then back for the next row, with the first woman poking a hole in the ground with every step and her partner dropping a seed into the hole and covering it with a push of her foot. Certainly, the work was easy, but they did it for 12 or more hours a day, day after day. During late spring and summer their days were spent with a hoe in hand, chopping weeds away from the cotton plants.

In August, watchmen were set to check the fields every day, waiting for the first bolls to open. The cotton bolls, which hold the fibers, are the seed pods, growing on the branches of the cotton plant. When the seeds are ripe, the boll bursts open, like a milkweed pod, and the cotton fiber is ready to be picked. At this point, every slave on the plantation, as young as 6 years old, was sent to the fields to pick cotton. There was a need for haste. Cotton, by its very nature, absorbs water. (Cotton clothes are comfortable for summer wear because the cloth soaks up the moisture from your skin and keeps you cool.) If it rains on an unpicked cotton field, the cotton absorbs the water like a sponge, the plant becomes heavy and falls down in the mud, and the crop is lost.

When picking cotton, slaves carried either a large wicker basket or a canvas sack. Wicker is made of sticks, woven together; the basket is awkward and heavy and scratches your arms. The canvas sack is also heavy, but at least it can be dragged behind, growing heavier as it collects dirt. Whatever you used, you picked as fast as your fingers could fly, because there was an overseer on a horse behind you, saying "Faster, faster!" and enforcing it with his whip. The cotton bolls have thorns on the end of each segment, which cut the hands, but the slaves could not take the time to pick carefully. They were told to wrap their hands in rags, so that the blood would not stain the cotton, and to keep on picking. An adult slave was expected to pick 200 pounds of cotton a day, - 200 pounds of fluff! If you didn't meet your quota, they beat you and, if they beat you so severely that you couldn't work the next day, they beat you again for not being able to work.

Once the crop was in, life was a little easier. The daily work now was combing the seeds from the cotton fibers, picking out any leaves and getting the harvest ready to be sent to market. Then came the time for repair or building projects on the plantation. If their master had no pressing work for them, he might hire out slaves to someone in need of temporary labor. There was seldom any rest time for a slave.

Life was not that much easier for slaves chosen to work in the house. Certainly, there were some old retainers who had raised their master and mistress from children and were devoted to them. These few were generally well treated; they were special and appreciated as such. Much more common was the footman who broke a dish and was beaten for it or the maid who had her face slapped by her mistress because she didn't move fast enough, or even because she looked her mistress in the eye. For female slaves there was always the danger of being chosen by the master as a "bed warmer". House slaves did at least have decent clothing (they would be seen by visitors) and enough to eat. They often tried to smuggle leftovers out to feed their families, but that was dangerous also, and punishments were severe. There was no penalty for a master who killed his slave, except the monetary loss. As far as the law was concerned, slaves were not considered citizens, - not even people. They were personal property of the master, like his wagon or his cow, and he could treat or dispose of them as he wished.

Soon the black slaves far outnumbered the white men in the south. A single plantation might own several hundred slaves, and the owners began to fear slave uprisings. The slaves were kept under guard at all times and the overseers became even more brutal. Laws were passed to make it illegal to teach a slave to read or write, as an educated slave would be even more dangerous. A miserable existence became even more unbearable.

Slaves often tried to escape from this tyranny. African-born slaves longed for the freedom they had once enjoyed and even the plantation-born slaves became desperate to find a life apart from the daily toil and whippings. But if he ran away, where could he go? He was given away by the color of his skin and was almost sure to be challenged by anyone who saw him. The few trusted slaves, who were sent on errands by themselves, carried passes which told who owned them and what time they were expected back. Without a pass, a slave found away from his plantation was in serious trouble. If he should manage to get far enough away that he couldn't be identified, a lawman or slave catcher would just sell him to another master. A few were befriended by the Seminole Indians in the Florida swamps or, if they could manage to reach Mexico, those Indian tribes also took in the fugitives. Almost all were apprehended and sent back to brutal punishment.

Slaves were told from childhood of the horrors that lay in store for anyone foolish enough to try to run away. The slave owners were determined that no slave ever be allowed to escape, as that would encourage others to try. Many plantations kept a pack of bloodhounds for the express purpose of tracking down fugitives. If the plantation owner and his overseers could not capture an escaped slave, they would post notices all over the county, describing the slave, telling who he belonged to and offering a reward for his return. That reward was almost always "dead or alive". If a slave catcher (bounty hunter) could catch a slave and drag him back in chains, he might earn $150. If he found his quarry but couldn't capture him, - if the man was too strong or too clever, - he wouldn't hesitate to shoot the slave and take the dead body back for half the posted reward. The dead man's body, displayed on the plantation, would prove that no one would be allowed to get away. That deterrent was worth half the reward.

Those captured and returned alive found their fate almost as bad. All slaves on the plantation were gathered to witness, and the returned slave would suffer in front of his family and friends. He would undoubtedly be whipped, often tortured. He might have an eye put out or be branded with a hot iron, often on the face. Sometimes toes would be cut off, the thinking being that it would now hurt too much to run, but that the slave could still hobble enough to work. The purpose was not so much that of punishing the returned slave as of instilling enough fear in the hearts of the onlookers that they would never dare try to escape themselves. The slave could also expect to be sold, as his owner understood that he had reached the desperate stage where he would try again for freedom if ever the opportunity presented itself.

A HAVEN IN CANADA

Finally, in 1793, Canada passed a law that any slave who reached Canada could live there in freedom and could even earn citizenship. This was probably not done with any higher humanitarian intention. Canada was a huge country with a very small population and badly needed to recruit more settlers. What's more, Canada was a British colony and their legislature would follow direction from England. Great Britain had lost their "American Colonies" some 20 years earlier, in a defeat that was still very hard for them to accept. They thought they would surely recapture that country soon, but first they would sow distrust and anger, to weaken the new republic. Already, the northern states had abolished slavery, and frustration was growing that the south would not do the same. The southerners insisted that slaves were essential to their way of life and had required that Thomas Jefferson remove a passage freeing all slaves before they would sign the Declaration of Independence. England hoped to divide north from south, an action that did not help them in the War of

1812, but which surely became part of the resentment leading to the Secession of the South and the Civil War.

The slaves did not learn of this new haven very quickly, especially as their masters tried to keep it from them. But gradually the news filtered in, often coming with the purchase of a new slave. Of course, the slaves could not speak of this openly, but it was whispered in the little cabins, and they had a novel way of spreading the news. They sang about it! The slaves had brought from Africa the tradition of singing while they worked. It helped time pass and kept them working together. In slavery there was nothing happy to sing about. Most of their songs were sad songs about dying and finding freedom in Heaven, - songs we refer to as Spirituals. They were mournful songs, often monotonous, and the overseers tuned them out. Thus they didn't pay attention when the slaves sang songs like "Follow the Drinking Gourd", which told of escape to Canada.

"When the sun comes back and the first quail calls,
Follow the drinking gourd.

For the old man is coming for to carry me to freedom,

Follow the drinking gourd."

This would not be comprehensible to white overseers, but it gave the slaves a dream. The "drinking gourd" was the Big Dipper, the constellation of stars that shows you the North Star. ('Dipper' was not a word the slaves used. Their dippers were the hollowed-out gourds they used to dip water and drink, a crooked-neck 'drinking gourd'.) If they could find the North Star and keep it ahead of them as they walked through the night, they could be sure of traveling north. "When the sun comes back" high in the sky after the winter and "the first quail calls", it's early March in the south, and the best time to slip away if you plan to run to freedom. The weather will be warm enough for you to live without shelter and you will have time to reach safety in Canada before winter comes again.

The "old man" carrying them to freedom was used in spirituals as a reference to God's coming to take them to Heaven, and would not have aroused suspicion. In this case it may have meant that an old man was coming in a wagon to take slaves to meet with the Underground Railroad, people who secretly helped slaves travel north, one night's travel at a time.

THE UNDERGROUND RAILROAD

And so we come to the Underground Railroad. It was neither underground nor a railroad. It was simply a very loosely connected group of people who were willing to help slaves escape from bondage and flee to Canada. The name comes from an occurrence at Ripley Ohio, along the Ohio River. A slave had escaped from his master and was running for the river. His master followed on a horse and arrived just in time to see the slave slip into the river and start to swim across. The owner rode up the river until he found a boat, which he took and followed in pursuit. He saw the slave climb out of the river and run up the bank into Ripley. He pulled his boat ashore and followed close behind, but he could not find the slave. No one had seen him and although he searched the small town all day, he finally had to go home, where he told people it was "as if the man had vanished underground onto a road which carried him away." The people who had hidden the slave thought this sounded pretty interesting. At that time, railroads were the newer, faster means of transportation, so the mysterious road became an "Underground Railroad", and they gave everything railroad terms.

The safe-houses became "stations" or depots", those who lived there were "stationmasters" or "agents", those who led or transported slaves on their nightly journeys were "conductors" and the slaves themselves were "passengers" or "packages". There is record of an ad placed in a Cincinnati newspaper, stating "Wanted: 2 tickets to Libertyville" (Libertyville was the Underground Railroad term for Canada), indicating that the one who placed the ad was hiding two fugitives and needed someone to come take them farther north.

There were highly principled people everywhere who wanted to help the slaves, but this was a very dangerous undertaking. According to the law, slaves were the personal property of their owners; thus a slave who tried to escape was stealing something valuable from his master; - he was trying to steal himself! This made the slave a thief and anyone who helped him was aiding and abetting a criminal. The Fugitive Slave Law of 1793 required the return of escaped slaves to their masters, no matter where in the United States they might be found. The slaves were not permitted to testify on their own behalf and the word of the slave owner or slave catcher was to be considered accurate. Of course, this led to great abuse, with free blacks being claimed unjustly and sold into slavery. Over the next half century, many northern states passed laws that hindered the enforcement of this law and infuriated the southerners. In 1850, Congress passed a new Fugitive Slave Law, commonly known as the Compromise Act, mainly in an attempt to quiet talk of secession from the southern states. This law reinforced the provisions of the original Fugitive Slave Law and strengthened the penalties for helping a fugitive escape. Lawmen who apprehended slaves were paid a bounty, and citizens who turned in a slave or notified the authorities of neighbors who broke this law were given a $5 reward for each slave retaken. Anyone caught breaking these laws could be sent to prison for up to 6 months and fined up to $1,000, a huge sum in those days. Anyone planning to help with the Underground Railroad needed to plan ahead and take many precautions.

Southerners who tried to help faced even greater reprisals. The plantation owners were furious that anyone would try to "steal their slaves away" and often took the law into their own hands. Southern agents or conductors faced having their barns or houses burned; they were often beaten, occasionally killed. In the south, the first contact was often an "old man" as noted in the song. An elderly person can get away with things the younger generation cannot. A young man, out driving his horse and wagon at midnight, would be watched with suspicion, if he stopped here and there at a thicket or crossroad. However an old man doing this would be given no more than an amused glance. An observer would say to himself that the poor old fellow had stayed too long with friends; maybe had a drop to drink, and now couldn't find his way home. In this way, he might stop at a crossroad, peer at the road signs, look up and down the road and wait long enough for someone to slip out of the shadows and slide into the wagon. He would then drive to the home of a friend, who would hide the slaves that night and the next day and take them a night's journey north the following night, hidden under hay or produce in his wagon.

Naturally, this was very dangerous, and a slave's chances of finding help were much greater once he crossed the Mason-Dixon Line and left slave territory. Most ran away on their own and found, or were found by, the Underground

Railroad later in their journey. A slave planning to flee did not have great preparations to make in advance. He could do little except wait for an opportunity to slip away unseen. His parents had taught him how to find the North Star, had told him that in Kentucky and Tennessee the rivers run north to the Ohio River and that moss grows on the north side of trees in the forest. They had told him to keep all the scraps of worn out clothes, as he would need layers in cooler weather. He might have hidden away a little bit of dried food, though there was never any extra food in the slave quarters. There was seldom much advance planning; most escapes were spur-of-the-moment. They often didn't even say goodbye to their loved ones, since they knew those left behind would be punished if the master thought they knew in advance.

One slave alone had the best chance of eluding the pursuers, but small family groups often attempted to flee together. Hardships were magnified for children, who could not be allowed to cry or even ask for reassurance. Silence and secrecy were their only hope. They had to travel at night and lie hidden during the daylight hours. They had to manage to live off the land, eating anything they could find. It was too dangerous to venture onto the roads; they had to go cross-country, scrambling over fences or rough ground in the dark. They had to stay well away from farm houses for fear a dog might bark and give them away. And there was always the danger that a bounty hunter was on your trail, led by a hound following your scent. They waded through streams to foil the hounds and slept in trees when they could find a thick, safe one.

The fugitive didn't know anything about the land he would be crossing. Most had never left the plantation before setting out. They couldn't read road signs if they saw them. They had no maps or directions. They just set off in the dark following the North Star. They didn't know about the mountains in Tennessee; they didn't know where they might find swamps. Could they dare to cross the bog or might they be dragged down by quicksand in the middle? If they had to retrace their steps, would they meet bounty hunters following them?

They did know about the Ohio River, which lay across their path if they were west of the Appalachians. They longed to reach that great river, even if it terrified them. Most slaves believed that they were safe once they crossed the river; they called it "crossing Jordan". After all, they were on free soil; Ohio was a free state and the residents couldn't keep slaves. Many were shocked to learn that they still had to reach Canada before they were safe from recapture. They also feared the river. Few were good swimmers. The slaves had grown up bathing in creeks or streams but had never had the leisure time to learn to keep themselves afloat in deep water. They would come upon the river in the dark and be faced with an ominous barrier across their path. If they had the time, they would search up and down the river, looking for a boat or raft they could take, but many had to go into the water with only a log to keep them afloat, and struggle to get across.

As the years passed, slaves heard that there were certain places where the Ohio River was less a challenge. This was long before the dams were built across the river to keep it consistently deep and navigable all year round. During the winter and spring it was a deep and rushing river but, in a dry August, it would become much more narrow and shallow. We now know that there were several fords on the Ohio, places where, in the summer, one could wade, ride or even drive a horse and wagon across the river. This may explain why by far the busiest crossing area was the short distance between

Ripley and Cincinnati, Ohio, a distance of only about 35 miles along the river.

Once they had crossed the river, slaves were much more likely to travel with the help of the Underground Railroad. Many people built their homes along the northern bank of the river to be in position to help fugitives as they crossed. One of these was the Reverend John Rankin. Born in North Carolina, he answered the call to the ministry and served parishes first in Tennessee and then in Kentucky. Although raised with slavery, he became convinced that it was an immoral practice and began to urge his parishioners to free their slaves. This was not a popular topic in Kentucky and the Rev. Rankin was first threatened and then actually forced to leave the state. He bought land on top of a hill overlooking the Ohio River at Ripley and kept candles burning in the windows every night, as a beacon to slaves on their flight to freedom. He and his family helped and hid countless fugitives, in spite of threats from the northern Kentucky slave owners.

Once the runaways became "passengers" on the "Railroad" their travels were much easier, though still dangerous. Hidden during the day in some small, secret hiding place, the fugitives were given good food and often warm clothing to replace their rags. At night, they were often hidden in a wagon, perhaps under a false bottom, and driven north for hours, to the home of another stationmaster, who would feed and hide them for the coming day. It was frightening and uncomfortable, but certainly better than living off the land and searching for hiding places. Some groups of slaves were led on foot to the next depot, if the conductor felt that was safer than using the more noisy and noticeable wagon. And often a stationmaster would simply tell the fugitives the path to their next safehouse and send them off with a clear description of the house where they would be welcomed before the next daybreak.

The stationmasters used signals to indicate safety or danger, but they were signals for the conductors and not slaves traveling on their own. Pursuing slave catchers would have discovered any signal common enough to be recognized by the slaves. The only sign we know to indicate a safehouse was a whitewashed chimney, especially one on the south side of a house. It was recognizable if the slaves were told to look for it and, as far as we know, was never discovered by the southerners. More common, and essential, was a signal which a station agent could put outside his house to indicate safety or danger to the conductor who might be bringing slaves to him. The two men who worked together would develop subtle signals to warn away the conductor if the agent were out of town, had company he couldn't trust or was afraid his house was being watched. He could not call his friend on the phone and say, "Not tonight". There had to be a signal he could put outside to warn the conductor to find somewhere else to take the slaves. It might be something like a candle burning in an upstairs window, a lantern hung on a certain branch of a tree or a cloth thrown over a bush. It could be a potted plant, which usually stood to the right of the door, moved to the left. It was often clothes left hanging on the line at night. (When you wash your clothes and hang them on the clothesline to dry, you always take them in before the sun goes down. If you do not, the dew falls and the clothes become too damp to put away.) In those days clothes, blankets or quilts left hanging on the line at night were either the sign of a careless housekeeper, who didn't get her laundry in on time, or they were a signal. Unfortunately, although the slave traveling alone might recognize this as a signal, he could not know if it meant safety or danger.

This amazing network led the slaves all the way to Canada. Slaves along the eastern seaboard were often transported by ship, hidden in the hold among the cargo they had loaded. They were kept hidden until they reached northern ports, where conductors waited to lead them north and across the border. Those who came from plantations along the Appalachian Plateau had a very dangerous trip north. This was a well-populated part of the country, with many villages and snake fences separating small farms, and it was hard to keep from being seen. There was little safety for them until they reached Pennsylvania. Many found help and guidance in Philadelphia, where many residents worked with the Underground Railroad.

Harriet Tubman is the heroine of that area. She had escaped from her master in Maryland and reached safety in Philadelphia, but she returned over and over, to bring to freedom all her family and many she did not know, often in dangerously large groups. She was a tough, no-nonsense leader. She made it clear that she would get to safety as many as possible but would not let anyone endanger the group. She would tell an old man who walked with a cane that she would leave him behind if he couldn't keep up. A mother with a new baby would be told that she must keep the child quiet or be left behind.

All those west of the Appalachians crossed the Ohio River into Ohio or Indiana and were led north. Many went to the Detroit area and crossed the Detroit River into Canada, but there were also routes that took them diagonally across the state, to cross into Canada near Niagara Falls. Other routes left them at the small port towns on Lake Erie, where intrepid sailors took them across the lake to Ontario in small sailboats.

SPRINGBORO

'Springborough', Ohio was founded in 1815 by Jonathan Wright, a Quaker from Pennsylvania. Jonathan was a well-to-do farmer and millwright, who had no great interest in what was then the Ohio frontier. However, Jonathan's father, Joel, was a surveyor and city planner who had been hired to lay out, or plat, the cities of Louisville, Kentucky and Columbus and Dayton in Ohio. While he was working in Dayton, Joel found the land south of town, still forest and almost untouched by the white man. Waynesville was a brand new town and Joel bought land for a farm near there and decided to settle down.

Then, as so often happens, Joel began urging his children to join him. Letters were sent, praising the beauty of the area and the opportunities for health and wealth. He missed his children; he wanted to watch his grandchildren grow up. He must have been persuasive because all of his children answered the plea and moved to the area between the Great and Little Miami Rivers. Jonathan gave in along with the rest. He sold his farm and his mills, packed up his family and moved west. Hoping to again have grist and woolen mills, the business he'd found so successful in Pennsylvania, he went looking for land to buy for his new home. He found the valley of Clear Creek, still owned by the government. It had been Indian land until a few years before. Besides Clear Creek it had Richards Run and Pleasant Valley Run, all good streams that Jonathan knew would turn a mill wheel. He bought the entire north side of the valley.

This area was almost entirely unsettled, and Jonathan saw that he would have no workers for his mills. So, drawing on his own surveying skills, he laid out his new town. There was only one building in the entire area he had bought, a house built by Griffy Griffis, on land he had never bothered to buy. When Jonathan bought the valley, Griffy had to buy his own house back from Jonathan. It cost him $300, and was probably 'highway robbery"! (This "Squatter's House", circa 1810, is still in place. It is now Springboro's Historical Museum.)

Jonathan laid out Main Street running north and south past the front of Griffy's house, where a trail already existed, and East Street parallel, to the east. He then added 7 cross streets, divided the blocks into lots and began selling lots to his family members, friends he coaxed into coming to join him and people who came soon to work in his mills. Friends urged Jonathan to name his town Wrightsville but Jonathan preferred Springborough, for all the springs in the valley. (The name Springborough was still in place in the 1830s; it was shortened to Springboro sometime later, but I have not been able to determine just when.)

Jonathan kept all the land beyond the alley west of Main Street. It was his farm and woodland and he built his big house on the only little hill in town, at what is now 80 West State Street. Quakers are expected to be humble and not try to appear important, but Jonathan was well-to-do and had a big family. His house was large and impressive, but with plain lines and no fancy touches, as a Quaker's house should be. (At some point, a stately front porch was added, but it would not have been in Jonathan's day). The house overlooked an expanse of prairie which reached half a mile to Clear Creek and was used as the general pasture for the entire town. His farm fields stretched to the west and remained agricultural land until the 1950s, when they became Springboro's first housing development, Royal Oaks, still known simply as "the plat".

This is a good time to say a few words about Quakers, or the Society of Friends. Quaker beliefs center on the "Inner Light", the innate goodness within a person which allows him to understand and follow the highly moral way he should conduct his life. Quakers are very introspective and avoid conditions which would take them away from this proper way of life. Thus, they consider themselves "plain" or "simple" people; they dress simply and their houses reflect the same lack of luxury. They are modest and do not wish to appear important. The Quaker community is important to them. As with the Wright family in Springboro, family members and friends stick together through the years. They believe strongly in the equality of all men and that it is their duty to help their fellow man in need. Naturally, Quakers were strongly opposed to slavery and, although otherwise very law abiding, were almost always ready to help the fugitive slave. (Quaker leader William Penn founded Philadelphia, "the city of brotherly love", and it remained largely Quaker through the years, which accounts for its being an Underground Railroad stronghold during these times.)

Springborough was a Quaker town. Most of the early residents were Jonathan's family or his acquaintances and their similar outlooks made for a comfortable community. The homes they built along Main Street were in the simple Quaker style, - plain, square buildings, built right on the sidewalk. (Back yards were practical for a barn, clothes lines, a garden or a few fruit trees; front yards were for show and the Quakers didn't need them.) Most were two story buildings. A business man had his shop or business on the first floor and the family lived upstairs. Most of these old buildings are still in place along Main Street, modernized indoors but looking much the same from the outside. Present day downtown Springboro is so similar in appearance to the village of the early 1800s that the entire original district has been recognized on the National Register of Historic Places.

TUNNELS AND HIDING PLACES

Naturally, a Quaker town being built at this time in this location was sure to see some activity with the Underground Railroad. The new town was just two night's travel from the Ohio River. Once across the river, a fugitive was very likely to find, or be found by, people eager to help him on his flight. The first conductor would lead him to a station in northern Hamilton County and his second night's travel would bring him to Springboro or Waynesville, Harveysburg, or Wilmington, - all Quaker towns, two night's travel from the river. Springboro's new residents built their houses to include places to hide slaves, planning in advance to be a part of this dangerous endeavor.

Jonathan's house, as almost all the early houses in town, was made of brick. There were no local sawmills or brick plants. The residents had their houses made of what was available. They could have a log house or they could make their own bricks. Most houses were built by first digging the basement and using that as a kiln to fire the bricks. There was plenty of clay along the streams. The bricks were formed, stacked in the dug-out basement and fired, by simply building a fire over and around them. Workers would build the walls in stages as the next batch of bricks baked.

Perhaps this extended building time encouraged the digging of tunnels between the houses. The owners would have had plenty of time to dig before the enclosing walls made it difficult to dispose of the excavated dirt. We know of 9 tunnels which were dug in Springboro: a few are documented and others are identified by physical evidence in the basements. There may well have been more, as these tunnels were not meant to be found. None still exist. They probably lasted as long as the traffic was only horses and buggies, but the coming of paving equipment, heavy trucks and fleets of school busses has collapsed every one.

Jonathan Wright built at least one tunnel from his basement and probably more. Jonathan's grandson, Fredrick, wrote about a tunnel, which ran from the basement to the home of a caretaker at the back of the property. He wrote that the slaves could run through the tunnel and that the caretaker would direct them down the hill to the stream, so that they could run through the water to elude pursuing hounds. During the early 1960's this house stood empty and became the local 'haunted house' to neighborhood children. Some of those, who found a way in and explored the basement, tell us that there were openings to 3 tunnels, the recorded one which ran north, one which ran west (probably to the barn) and one which ran east, toward Main Street.

Jonathan also had a hidden room built into his house. It is the only one we know of which still exists, though probably every safe-house had a hiding place. This is a small, triangular room above the attic stairway, accessible only through a trap door in the attic floor. It has no level floor. Anyone hidden in that room would have had to climb down the ladder, which is still there, fastened to the wall with pegs, and stand on the ladder. It would have held three people at the most. Whoever hid them would close them in, cover the trap door with a rug or piece of furniture and leave them trapped. It would have been very frightening and claustrophobic, but they only had to stay hidden long enough for the intruder to search the house and then they would be released.

Springboro was a doubly safe place for slaves, as about a third of its population was made up of freed slaves, mostly from Virginia. Virginia state law required freed slaves to leave the state within a week. Most went west in search of a new life and many of those who came to Springboro stayed. The Quakers accepted them without question and there was always work in Jonathan's mills. Fugitives were much less visible in this integrated environment, and the black families would hide them in plain sight and introduce them as visiting relatives. Jonathan would urge them to stay for a while, if they felt safe in doing so. He would put them to work in his mills, so that they would earn a little money to help them get started in Canada, and he would hire someone to teach them to read and write.

TOURING MAIN STREET

Springboro's historic tours start at the Springboro Area Historical Society's Museum, 110 South Main St, where visitors hear much of the information you have read here and are shown the displays in the Underground Railroad Room. The next stage takes us down Main Street to learn about a few of the old houses we know were Underground Railroad stations. We have already visited the Jonathan Wright House, now a Bed and Breakfast, where you may spend the night in a beautifully furnished bedroom and look through a small window in the closet to examine the interior of Jonathan's hidden room.

Before we go, let's say a word about our little Museum. This is the "Squatter's House", which I mentioned earlier, predating Jonathan Wright's coming by several years. Before anyone lived in this part of the valley, Griffy Griffis decided this was a good spot to build. With so much unoccupied land, why not put his house here, along the track from Cincinnati to Dayton? We think he may have been a blacksmith, which would explain the building all by itself, along the trail. If you look at the building from the front, you can see that it consists of one room parallel to the road and one, set back, at right angles to it. Check the roof line on that side room; - it's off center. We think that was probably a separate building originally, with an overhanging roof on the south side, perfect for a smithy. The front room was probably only the southern portion at first, with the northern third added later. You can see the difference in the foundation and in the brick pattern.

I also often mention the oval 'circa' plaques. These are meant to tell the approximate date when the building was built ('circa' is Latin for 'around'). It's very hard to tell exactly how old these original buildings are. The usual method is to go back to the records of property values for tax purposes.

When the value of the land went up considerably, it usually meant a house had been built on that lot. When the Historical Society first offered these plaques to the property owners, the date recorded was what the owners told us. Unfortunately, some of those owners hadn't done the research and so there are a few of these plaques that are even too far off for 'circa'. However, we think most of the early ones are accurate.

The bronze historical plaques appear in front of the sites and buildings that are recognized as property of Underground Railroad conductors, and other historically important buildings. The City of Springboro had these produced and installed, having worked with the Historical Society to make sure this information is accurate. The plaques add a great deal to our Historic District and make self-guided walking tours practical and instructive.

NAPOLEON JOHNSON

As we leave the Museum, I may mention the house just to the north, (100 S. Main St) as it was one of several houses owned by Napoleon Johnson. Napoleon was a slave, freed by his master in Virginia. When he found that his wife was not also to be given her freedom, he at first refused to leave, but his wife convinced him that at least one of them should know freedom. Napoleon came west to Springboro, where he went to work as a plasterer and saved every penny. In less than two years, he was able to return to Virginia and buy freedom for not only his wife, but his wife's mother as well, and bring them back to Springboro with him. They lived in a small cabin and continued to save much of the money he made. Freed slaves were not allowed to own property, but Napoleon had

48

trusted friends who bought several houses on his behalf, which he was able rent out, allowing his family to live quite comfortably. Napoleon enlisted and fought for the Union during the Civil War. He is buried in The Friends Cemetery on Factory Street.

JONAH THOMAS

Jonah Thomas' house is less than a block from the Museum (200 S. Main St.). It is a tall brick house on the street corner. If you do not consider the frame addition, added later to the back, you will see how compact the original building was. We don't know where slaves were hidden here, but it doesn't look big enough for a family of 4, let alone any kind of hidey-hole. Jonah was a harness maker and the downstairs was his harness shop. He, his wife Hannah and two sons, Ira and Alfred, lived upstairs. It's no wonder that several years later they sold this house and moved into a larger one just across the street (205 S. Main St.) where, again, they lived upstairs over the harness shop.

Slaves were hidden in both houses. John Van Zandt, from Hamilton County, brought them at night, hidden beneath a false bottom in his wagon, and left them with Jonah. Jonah hid them all the next day and the following night he, or one of his sons, would take them in his wagon to the home of Dr. Abraham Brooks, east of Harveysburg. This was traveling east rather than north, to detour around Dayton, a dangerous city for the Underground Railroad. Slaves traveling on their own were warned to stay well to the east of the towns along the Great Miami River, and most routes from Springboro went to the east of Dayton, sending the slaves north through Xenia and Yellow Springs.

In those days, mills were always built along the rivers, since they ran on water power. Then, as still today, Kentuckians came north to work in the mills and those Kentuckians were a threat to the Underground Railroad. Having grown up with slavery, they considered the practice right and proper, and thought that it was terrible to have these northerners encouraging their slaves in flight. Any time they could, they would catch fugitives and send them south or try to catch the conductors in action.

John Van Zandt was caught by the law one night on his way to Springboro with a load of slaves in his wagon. The slaves were sent back to their owners and Mr. Van Zandt had to appear in court. He admitted to transporting fugitive slaves (he'd been caught red-handed) but wouldn't tell where he was taking them, and so the connection to Springboro was not discovered. There is no record of any slave being retaken while under the care of Springboro's conductors.

Mr. Van Zandt had a lenient judge, was let off with a fine, and was probably soon transporting slaves again. The conductors were dedicated to their cause and persevered through danger and hardship. There is a record of a Cincinnatian who, upon being released from prison, once again, said, "I have nothing left. I am penniless and my family has left me, but you may be sure that I will go out and help the first poor fugitive I can find."

It has been estimated that 200,000 slaves attempted to flee to Canada in the 67 years before the end of the Civil War finally ended slavery in the United States. Of those about half, or 100,000, were successful. Probably 40,000 passed through Ohio. In Springboro's 50 years of activity, we may conservatively estimate that its conductors protected some 2,500 fugitives and helped them on their way to freedom.

JOSEPH STANTON

Less than a block south of Jonah's home is the Joseph Stanton house (250 S. Main St.). We call this the 'Quilt House', since Springboro folklore says that Joseph used to hang a quilt on the line, in the back yard if all was well, and right up at the front if there were danger. ('Folklore' refers to stories that are passed down by word of mouth through the generations. There is often no proof for these stories, but they are usually accepted as being based on fact and are often accepted in support of physical evidence.) The small brick building just north of the house was the family's springhouse, built around one of the many springs that gave the town its name, and was used like a refrigerator, to keep food cool and fresh.

In the basement, between two sidewalk-level windows, is a bricked-in doorway, which would have led out under the front sidewalk. We're almost sure that it was the entrance to a tunnel, which ran under Main Street to the building on the vacant lot opposite. This was an apothecary shop or drug store, and was also said to be a safe-haven for slaves. If someone came to search either building, slaves could run through the tunnel and escape through the building across the street.

Joseph's uncle, James Stanton, who lived just north of town, was also a dedicated abolitionist. Both Stantons came from Dinwiddie County, Virginia. When living in Virginia, James has been active in working, through the courts, to arrange the emancipation of all Virginia slaves who carried Native American blood. After moving to Springboro he continued seeking freedom for slaves. He made several trips to Virginia, bringing back as many as 20 slaves each time. Some he bought, some probably came on false papers and a few might have been just hidden in with the others. Those he had bought were then free to either stay in Springboro or travel the Underground Railroad to Canada with the others.

THE DECKER HOUSE

To make this corner even more interesting, the building on the southwest corner, across State Street (305 S. Main St.), has a section of the basement wall adjacent to State Street which has clearly been rebuilt, probably to close the entrance to another tunnel connecting to the apothecary shop. When the interior of this house was remodeled, about 20 years ago, a room in the attic was found to have a double wall. It had enough space within the wall for people to slide in and stand in this hidden space. It probably had a hidden door for access that would have been invisible behind an open door to the room.

The barn behind this house was the livery stable for the town. Horses could be stabled here and Mr. Decker ran a carriage route to Franklin on a regular schedule, - a horse-drawn bus line.

SPRINGBOROUGH'S CITY HALL

Midway down the block, at 325 S. Main St, we find the small building that now houses the Chamber of Commerce. Until the 1940s this served as Springboro's City Hall, a small building for a small town. The door on the north was originally a large barn door, as this side housed the town fire engine, first a horse-drawn vehicle and later a Model T. The fire siren is still in place on the roof. The south side had one room for business or meetings and three jail cells ran across the back, so whatever law enforcement the City had must have been headquartered here also.

The "town pump" was at the edge of the street just to the south of this building, with a horse trough beside it. It supplied water for anyone who didn't have a well of his own.

JEREMIAH STANSEL

The end of the block brings us to the Jeremiah Stansel House (350 S. Main St.), which he built for his new bride when he married. Springboro folklore tells us he built a tunnel which ran for over a block, from the back of his house past East Street, opening over the hill above Richards Run, but no sign of it remains. Jeremiah evidently admired the house across Main Street, as he built his from the same plans. This is still quite noticeable if you stand in front of them and compare.

Jeremiah was born in Boonesborough Stockade in Kentucky, moving with his family to the Springboro area at a young age. His father's story is interesting. Henry Stansel was born in a frontier settlement in Pennsylvania. When he was about 6 years old, Indians raided his farm, killing his father and older brothers and carrying Henry off with them. He was raised with the Indian boys, becoming as capable as they at finding game or following a trail. When he was 16, French Canadian traders found him and convinced the Indians to let him return to his family.

Life in a more civilized Pennsylvania settlement soon became boring for Henry and he set out for the west, settling at Boonesborough, KY, where he became close friends with Daniel Boone and Simon Kenton. When Daniel Boone's daughter was kidnapped by Indians, it was these three men who went in pursuit and rescued the girl. After he moved his family to Springboro, his two frontier friends visited Henry more than once and we are told they also visited Jeremiah's house on Main Street.

Another bit of Springboro folklore links Jeremiah with Mahlon Wright, Jonathan's son. These two young men were on their way to Lebanon one day when they came across a man leading a coffle of slaves on his way to Missouri. (Although Ohioans could not own slaves, it was lawful to transport them through the state. There was even a major slave market in Cincinnati.) The two young Quakers knocked the man down and released the slaves, telling them that they were free. The slaves fled in all directions. The furious slave trader filed charges in Lebanon against Jeremiah and Mahlon and they were arrested and taken there. He also had been annoyed when passing through Springboro to see a prosperous-looking free black man named Fred Wilson. He spitefully charged Fred with having stolen money from him, which was not true. Fred was arrested and taken to Franklin for trial.

Slave traders didn't find much sympathy in Warren County and Jeremiah and Mahlon got off with a slap-on-the-wrist fine. On their return to Springboro, however, they heard about Fred's arrest and were worried, with good reason. Franklin was one of those river towns with many former Kentuckians and Monroe, just a few miles to the south, was headquarters for a group known as The Knights of the Golden Circle. This organization was to become one of the founding segments of the Ku Klux Klan after the Civil War. This was not a safe place for Fred.

Fred's trial had ended with his acquittal, but a mob had gathered and threatened to burn down the jail if Fred weren't turned over to them. Just as the jailer was about to give Fred to the mob to save himself, a group of the young Springboro Quakers rode up, armed with their hunting rifles. They got Fred on a horse and told him to ride for his life while they held off the mob. Fred crossed the river and rode well north before circling back to Springboro and safety.

Another story about Fred Wilson is recounted in a letter. Fred and the letter writer were doing repairs on the road west of Springboro, when they found a man camped along the road with 10 slaves. The man offered to buy Fred, and his companion replied that Fred was not a slave. Fred muttered under his breath, "His'n won't be for long, either". That evening the slave trader went to have dinner with a hospitable neighbor and returned to find the slaves freed from their shackles and gone. Fred had also disappeared; he led his charges all the way to Canada.

WARNER BATEMAN

Across Factory Street from the Jeremiah Stansel House is the Warner Bateman House (400 S. Main St.). Warner and his brother John were nephews of Jonathan Wright's wife, Mary. When they joined the rest of the clan in Springboro, the brothers bought 3 of the 4 lots in this block. Warner built his beautiful big house (again, the porch would not have been original) on this corner and John built his house among the trees farther down the block. The family business was on the south corner, next to John's house, where "the K" now stands. The family business was a tannery, where animal hides were turned into leather, and this seems like a strange neighbor, not suitable for any residential district. The tanning process required that the hides be soaked for six weeks in large vats filled with water, to which had been added the bark of any of the nut trees. The bark of the walnut, hickory or chestnut trees all contain tannin, a chemical which helps to break down the fibers in the hides and make the leather soft and pliable. The hides were taken out of the vat once a week, put on the ground and scraped, to remove the flesh from one side and the hair from the other, and then returned to the vat. This was before the coming of window screens, air conditioning or much understanding of sanitary practice. Imagine the mess, the flies and the smell!

And yet, the tannery sheltered many run-away slaves through the years. As a safe-house, the tannery had many benefits, and the fugitives were quite willing to tolerate the smell for the security. Bounty hunters seldom bothered to search there; they didn't care to dig around in piles of uncured cowhides, looking for someone who probably wasn't there. If they asked their hounds to find the slaves' scent, the dogs were so distracted by the scent of the hides that they were of no use. A man-made ditch, known as a 'race', brought in the water for the tanning process and carried it away, to drain over the hill into Richards Run. The slaves liked this watery trail to help them get a head start on tracking hounds. And finally, there was the added safety of a tunnel under South Street, which connected the tannery to its business offices on the south side of the street. We know this tunnel was still open in the 1920s. Springboro school records from 1924 tell of taking children on a field trip to walk through the tunnel under South Street.

Warner Bateman became a federal judge and as such would have taken an oath to uphold the laws of the United States. Good Quaker that he was, Warner evidently decided that God's laws were more important than man's laws, because he and John both hid slaves in their own houses as well as in the tannery.

Physical evidence in the house catty-corner from The K, at 505 S. Main, suggests that it may also have had a tunnel from the northeast corner of the basement. It may have led to the house to the north of South St. or possibly to the Tannery, but we will probably never know.

THE FRIENDS' CEMETERY

Half a block west of Warner Bateman's house, on Factory St, is the Friends' Cemetery, Springboro's original cemetery. This lovely spot serves as the final resting place for at least 8 Underground Railroad conductors. There is only one discernable family plot here, that of Jonathan Wright, his parents, his family and several generations of descendants. The raised structure is a monument to the family, with the names engraved in the stone surface. It was installed by Jonathan's great grandchildren and probably would have embarrassed Jonathan, as it isn't in keeping with the modest Quaker purpose. However, it is nice for us to be able to read the family tree of Springboro's founder.

The cemetery appears to have very few graves, though it is, in fact, quite full. The Meeting House stood in the southeast corner, with a parking lot for the horses and buggies along the eastern fence line. There are graves among the trees, and along the south fence is a row of children's graves. Just a few years after the town's founding, an epidemic of some sort took many of the children, who were all buried in a row. There are 13 black residents buried here also, including Napoleon Johnson. The quiet and introspective Quaker religion is seldom the choice of African Americans, but here are several who stayed with the Quakers in death as they had in life. The original headstones are either flat on the ground or only about 8" high, in the style of the 'plain people'. As the restrictions eased in later generations, we find the rounded tombstones from the late 1800s and the polished stones from the 1900s.

The open area along Factory Road is also full of graves. If you look closely, you can see that there is a little roll to the ground, showing the rows of graves running east and west. At one time this cemetery was abandoned and grew up in brush. In the 1960s, two Boy Scout troops adopted as a project the cemetery clean-up. They cut down and hauled away the scrub trees and bramble bushes. They tried to mow the grass but broke their mower blades on all the rocks, so they hauled away the rocks also, not realizing that the Quakers often used a plain, flat fieldstone to mark the head of a grave. Although all the graves in this section are unmarked, we have, at the Museum, a beautifully hand-written list of who is buried in every grave. There is one exception. Grave 7 in row 7 is simply marked "Unknown". It's rather unusual to have a grave in a cemetery that is not identified in any way. We have an explanation for this case in Springboro's folklore.

As the story goes, an elderly slave knocked on the door of the house at 660 South Main Street late one night and begged to be hidden, as he was being closely followed by a bounty hunter. The residents took him in and hid him in their secret hiding place. This was at the back of a closet, where a board could be pulled up in the wall, allowing someone to crawl behind it and lie in the wall. The board was then lowered to hide him. By the time the slave was hidden, the bounty hunter was pounding on the door, demanding to be let in. The law in those days said that, when a bounty hunter came to town, he had to get a permit to search from the local police or sheriff. This permit then required that residents allow the slave catcher to come in and search their houses, looking for fugitive slaves. The bounty hunter was admitted and searched the house, but couldn't find the slave hidden in the closet. Unfortunately, the bounty hunter had seen the slave at the door of the house and knew he was there. He informed the residents that if they didn't give the slave up to him, he would send for the sheriff. Since they would not give up the slave, the people were arrested and taken to Lebanon. The next morning, the judge threw the case out of court, since the bounty hunter could not produce any evidence, and set the residents free. They hurried back to Springboro but found that the old slave had died in the closet overnight. They now had a different problem. If they called the undertaker, it would be obvious that they had hidden a fugitive and they would be arrested again, with clear evidence against them. So they got their family together, smuggled the body out of the house that night and buried it in the next space in the cemetery. We think the old slave is probably the 'unknown' in grave 7, row 7.

THE NULL HOUSE

Our final stop on the tour is at the Null Log House in Heatherwoode subdivision. This two story log house is the oldest structure on its original site in Warren County. It was built in 1798 by Christian and Charles Null from Virginia, who came to claim land owed to Christian for his army service during the Revolutionary War. At the start of the war, Christian's older brother Joshua joined "Light-horse" Henry Lee's cavalry and went to fight for independence. A year later, when his comrades brought Joshua's body home for burial, Christian, in sorrow and anger, joined in his brother's place. He was 12 years old. Very few of the American soldiers were paid during that war; the young government could hardly afford to feed them, let alone pay them. In the last decade of the century, the soldiers were still wondering when, or if, they would be paid.

At this time, southern Ohio was still Indian Territory. The land was forest, with occasional patches of prairie, mostly on the tops of the hills. It has been said that the forest was so thick that a squirrel could go up a tree at Marietta and start running west through the trees and not have to come down until he was halfway across Indiana. This was the Indians' best hunting land, rich in all kinds of game, and they guarded it jealously. Kentucky had been settled a decade earlier and now a few people were crossing the river, building cabins and clearing the land for crops. The Indians resented this incursion; they burned the cabins and the crops and ran the settlers back across the river. The settlers appealed to the government, which sent in the army and, after several years of fighting, the Indians were defeated at the Battle of Fallen Timbers and, in the Treaty of Greenville (1795), agreed to move north or west and leave southern Ohio open for settlement.

The government was eager to move settlers into the area, so that the Indians would not try to return, and so announced that they would give land in Ohio to the veterans of the Revolutionary War in payment of their debt. To receive payment, the veterans had to come to Ohio, claim their land in an amount determined by their years of service, and build a house. They could not sell their land until it had a house ready to be occupied. Christian had served for many years and was owed too much money to ignore this opportunity. He had to go to Ohio and build a house. So he and his older brother Charles loaded all the tools and supplies they would need onto pack horses (there were few roads in the Ohio Territory) and set off to the west.

When they reached the Ohio River, they camped for a few days on the river bank, until a flatboat came floating down the river. Many people who came to settle in southern Ohio or northern Kentucky went to Pittsburgh, where they built or bought a big flat-bottomed boat, often large enough to transport many families with all their worldly goods. They loaded their animals, tools and furniture in the hold, camped out on the deck, pushed off from the bank and let the current carry them down the river. When they found a place for their new settlement, they pulled the boat ashore, unloaded it, took the boat apart and used the lumber to build their houses. That's known as American ingenuity!

The Null brothers flagged down a big boat and asked for a lift. The men said "No room!" but the women thought two strong young men might be handy to have along, and so the Nulls, with their horses and equipment, piled aboard. The women were right. Several days later a thunderstorm burst overhead with such violence that the animals in the hold panicked and one kicked a board loose. The river was rushing in and the boat was in danger of sinking. It was Christian who organized the frightened settlers to bail and went over the side, with a rope around his waist, to pound the board back into place.

Opposite Maysville, KY, the Nulls left the boat and started north, looking for the best place for their new home. This hilltop seemed to have all they needed, so they stopped here. This was a high point, which was good for a frontiersman or a farmer. The frontiersman could see campfire or chimney smoke and keep track of who was where in his world. The farmer could see storms coming in time to get his crops or livestock under cover. They had a good water supply. Clear Creek is only a quarter of a mile down the hill but, even better, there was a spring just over the edge of the hill, and even a spring in the cellar they dug! (It was there until the golf course was built and the construction equipment cut into the aquifer.) The brothers may have noticed sycamore trees on the hilltop and known they would find water without having to dig a deep well. (There is a sycamore growing just beside the parking area.) Sycamores usually grow along streambeds; they like to have their roots wet. The house was built right beside the "road". The main east-west Indian trail ran across this hilltop, right through the present parking space.

The Nulls rode to Cincinnati to register their claim and then started building. The top of the hill was probably one of those bits of open prairie, but they undoubtedly had plenty of woodland also. Everything had to be done by hand. They cut down the trees with axes, squared them up with axes and notched the corners so that the logs fit snugly together. (The ax marks are still visible on the original upper logs. The lower logs are more recent replacements.) They probably dragged the logs to the house site using their horses and lifted them into place using pulleys and horsepower. They "chinked" the

73

spaces between the logs with a mixture of sand, clay and horsehair. The original roof would have been covered with shingles chipped out of a cedar log. The windows probably didn't have glass for several years, until Cincinnati became a big enough city that they floated glass down the river from Pittsburgh. The windows would have had heavy shutters and been covered with animal hides to keep out the weather. The Null brothers were not house builders, - they were farmers -, but they knew enough about building to erect a house which has stood for over 200 years!

This was one of the first houses in the county. It must have been a lonely year for the brothers and they must have hoped to see travelers on the road past their door. When the house was almost completed, they heard a dog barking one evening. In great excitement, they saddled their horses and rode west, following the sound. They found a new house going up where Franklin now stands, - their closest neighbor.

The original house had one room downstairs and an upstairs room the same size, probably divided into three bedrooms. (The two wings were built by the second owner, some 35 years later.) There is an attic above, about 5' high at the peak of the roof. The first floor has a massive fireplace and each of the other 2 floors has a tiny fireplace that opens into a different flue in the same chimney. That main fireplace would have been the center of life in this house. It not only provided all the heat in the house, but was also where the meals were cooked and the main source of light after dark. The Nulls might have brought kerosene lanterns, but they would have had to ride to Cincinnati to get kerosene. They would have made their own candles from animal fat, but would have used them sparingly. They probably just went to bed soon after the sun went down.

When the house was completed, the brothers went back to Virginia, helped sell the farm and pack up all their belongings, and brought their families west to the frontier. Nine people moved into this house. Christian wasn't yet married, but Charles had a wife and 4 children, the youngest less than 6 months old when they left the comparative comfort and safety of their farmhouse in Virginia. Their parents came also. The children probably slept in the attic. It would have been miserably hot in the summer and cold in the winter, but frontier kids were hardy. A year later, Charles built his own house, a duplicate of this, about half a mile away, and moved his family there.

Thirty five years later, the second owner, Jeremiah Taylor, who had married one of Christian Null's daughters, added the two wings to the house and built the basement under the north end of the house. He also built a huge barn which stood to the southwest of the house and which was demolished in 1993, in spite of the Springboro Historical Society's efforts to save it. Mr. Taylor had a flair for the grand look. His barn was probably one of the largest in the state. A four-story bank barn, it was built with a ramp and bridge to the main door, like a moated castle entrance. The third level floors only extended one third of the way from the side walls, leaving the central section open. Mr. Taylor used to boast that he could drive his fully loaded hay wagon into the barn and turn it around inside, by swinging his team of horses under the third floor while keeping the wagon in the center of the barn.

The two small wings of the house were built in 1832. During the rebuilding in 1994, a board was removed from the south wing. On the inside, in pencil, is written "Springborough, Warren County, 1832", so we know when this addition took place. The north side of the house probably had a small cave dug under the foundation, as a "root cellar", for storing perishables. Mr. Taylor enlarged this area as he built the north wing above, making this a real cellar, with a sloping "cellar door" and stone steps down from the back porch. The walls were dry-laid stone, - flat stones chosen to fit tightly together and pushed into the dirt, without any mortar to hold them in place. The rafters were simply trees, with the bark still in place, smoothed on one side to accommodate nailing on the floor boards. These logs with the bark left on are surprising, but Mr. Taylor knew what he was doing. After 175 years in a damp environment, these rafters show very little deterioration, but the one squared-up log, which he used as a cross-brace, is rotting away and so soft that you can push a fingernail into it. In a finishing touch tribute to his love of the grand style, he put a herring-bone pattern brick floor in his cellar!

Unusual as these features are, the things that especially interest us are the two small openings high up in the south wall, leading to the space under the center of the house. There is no logical reason for these "windows", as any opening weakens the stability of the dry-laid wall. The space under the house is too damp for storage and there was no need for access to plumbing or electrical installation at the time this was built. The foundation of the house was loose stone. If someone needed to get under the house he could move a few stones and crawl in. We theorize that these opening provided a hiding place for fugitive slaves.

Descendants of the Null family tell us that this did serve as a safe-house for the Underground Railroad. The residents were not actively involved, but they did take in run-aways who came seeking shelter. Fugitives could be hidden in the cellar with the door locked behind them. Anyone looking for them would have to knock on the door and ask to search. The knocking and voices from upstairs would be easily heard by anyone hidden in the cellar, giving him plenty of time to scramble through the opening and back under the house, where he could hide beyond the floor joists and out of sight. A bounty hunter might suspect that someone was under the house, but how would he get him out? He wouldn't have enough light to see more than about three feet into the darkness. His only option would have been to crawl under, groping in the dark crawlspace. He would not like this idea, knowing that his prey was probably waiting, armed with one of the many rocks that litter the floor. In the end, this was probably a rather safe hiding place.

There may have been a second hiding place in the old house. We're told by people who used to live here, that there was a small space beneath the floor of the north wing, accessible through a concealed door over the cellar stairs. That space is not visible now, but may have been covered over with renovation of the building.

The Null House is owned by the City of Springboro and is furnished and managed by the Springboro Area Historical Society. When Heatherwoode was being developed, the Historical Society was founded, for the purpose of seeing that the log house remained on its rightful site atop the hill, overlooking Springboro. For two years, the group worked to counteract attempts to move or demolish the old building, through all legal and political methods available. In the end, the Society was able to reach an agreement with the developer and the City, with the result that this treasure remains, to teach the present generation about life in the earliest days of Ohio. It was restored by 3 Society members, Charlie Logan, Gil Morris and Paul Travisano, who worked for nearly a year to replace time and weather damaged logs and return the old house to a structure in which all Springboro takes pride.

Notes:

Notes:

www.ingramcontent.com/pod-product-compliance
Lightning Source LLC
Chambersburg PA
CBHW031328040426
42443CB00005B/261